Rookie
Read-About® Holidays

Independence Day

D0094131

By David F. Marx

Consultant
Katharine A. Kane, Reading Specialist
Former Language Arts Coordinator
San Diego County Office of Education

Children's Press®
A Division of Grolier Publishing
New York   London   Hong Kong   Sydney
Danbury, Connecticut

Visit Children's Press® on the Internet at:
http://publishing.grolier.com

Designer: Herman Adler Design Group
Photo Researcher: Caroline Anderson

Library of Congress Cataloging-in-Publication Data

Marx, David F.
    Independence Day / by David F. Marx.
        p. cm. — (Rookie read-about holidays)
    Includes index.
    Summary: Introduces the history of Independence Day and explains
how it is celebrated today.
        ISBN 0-516-22232-5 (lib. bdg.)   0-516-27176-8 (pbk.)
        1. Fourth of July—Juvenile literature. 2. Fourth of July celebrations—
Juvenile literature. [1. Fourth of July. 2. Holidays.] I. Title. II. Series.
E286.M35   2001
394.2634—dc21
                                                                00-026856

It's the Fourth of July!
Can you guess whose
birthday it is?

The Fourth of July is the birthday of the United States of America.

We call this holiday Independence Day.

The United States Capitol

Independence means freedom. On Independence Day, we remember when the United States became a free country.

That was the beginning of the country, or its birthday.

More than two hundred years ago, the United States was not yet a country.

A king ruled the people who lived there. The king was in England, a country across the Atlantic Ocean.

The king sent his army to the United States.

Some of the men who met in Philadelphia

In 1776, fifty-six men met in Philadelphia, Pennsylvania.

They agreed that England should not rule over them.

They decided that America should be its own country.

These men signed
the Declaration of
Independence.

Have you ever heard
of Thomas Jefferson?
He wrote the Declaration
of Independence.

The Declaration of Independence declared, or said, that the United States of America was free from England.

The Declaration was dated July 4, 1776. So the Fourth of July became the birthday of the United States.

DECLARATION OF INDEPENDENCE

In Congress 4th July. 1776.

Every year on Independence Day, Americans celebrate their nation's birthday with huge parties.

Here is a celebration from more than one hundred years ago.

In some towns, Fourth of July morning starts with a big pancake breakfast.

Independence Day parties
are always decorated in
America's special colors:
red, white, and blue.
These are the colors
of the American flag.

Many towns have
Independence Day parades.

Some people carry
American flags as they
march down the street.

The nation's birthday party lasts into the night.

People gather in parks and have picnics. They wait for the sun to set.

Then it's time for
fireworks! What a great
way to end a holiday.

Fireworks by the Statue of Liberty

Fireworks are pretty, but they are also very loud!

Fireworks are just another way to shout, "Happy Birthday, United States!"

Words You Know

American flag

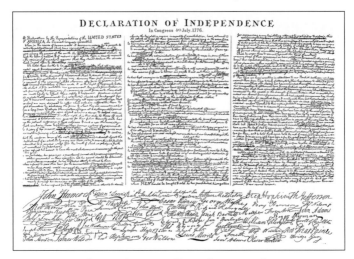

Declaration of Independence

fireworks

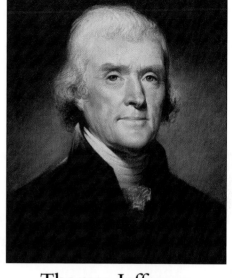

Thomas Jefferson

parade

Index

About the Author

David F. Marx is an author and editor of children's books. He resides in the Chicago area.

Photo Credits